U.S. WARS

THE CIVIL WAR

A MyReportLinks.com Book

Kim A. O'Connell

MyReportLinks.com Books

an imprint of

Enslow Publishers, Inc.

Box 398, 40 Industrial Road
Berkeley Heights, NJ 07922
USA

MyReportLinks.com Books, an imprint of Enslow Publishers, Inc. MyReportLinks is
a trademark of Enslow Publishers, Inc.

Library of Congress Cataloging-in-Publication Data

O'Connell, Kim A.
  The Civil War / by Kim A. O'Connell.
     p. cm. — (U.S. wars)
Summary: An overview of the Civil War which includes Internet links to
web sites.
Includes bibliographical references and index.
  ISBN 0-7660-5130-7
  1. United States—History—Civil War, 1861–1865—Juvenile literature.
[1. United States—History—Civil War, 1861–1865.] I. Title. II.
Series.
E468.O26 2003
973.7—dc21

                              2002014757

Printed in the United States of America

10 9 8 7 6 5 4 3 2 1

To Our Readers:
Through the purchase of this book, you and your library gain access to the Report Links that specifically back
up this book.
The Publisher will provide access to the Report Links that back up this book and will keep these Report Links
up to date on **www.myreportlinks.com** for three years from the book's first publication date.
We have done our best to make sure all Internet addresses in this book were active and appropriate when we
went to press. However, the author and the Publisher have no control over, and assume no liability for, the
material available on those Internet sites or on other Web sites they may link to.
The usage of the MyReportLinks.com Books Web site is subject to the terms and conditions stated on the
Usage Policy Statement on **www.myreportlinks.com**.
A password may be required to access the Report Links that back up this book. The password is found on the
bottom of page 4 of this book.
Any comments or suggestions can be sent by e-mail to comments@myreportlinks.com or to the address on
the back cover.

Photo Credits: © Corel Corporation, pp. 1 (background), 3; © MyReportLinks.com Books, p. 4;
Defense Visual Information Center/National Archives and Records Administration, pp. 1, 16, 22, 28,
37, 39, 42; Library of Congress, pp. 11, 33, 34, 44; PBS, *The Civil War*, p. 12; The Gilder Lehrman
Institute of American History/The Chicago Historical Society, pp. 15, 20, 24, 30; U.S. Department of
the Interior, pp. 19, 26, 31, 38.

Cover Photo: Painting: *First at Vicksburg*, H. Charles McBarron, Courtesy of the National Museum
of the U.S. Army; **Photographs:** Grant and Lee, Courtesy of the Library of Congress.

Contents

MyReportLinks.com Books
Great Books, Great Links, Great for Research!

MyReportLinks.com Books present the information you need to learn about your report subject. In addition, they show you where to go on the Internet for more information. The pre-evaluated Report Links that back up this book are kept up to date on **www.myreportlinks.com**. With the purchase of a MyReportLinks.com Books title, you and your library gain access to the Report Links that specifically back up that book. The Report Links save hours of research time and link to dozens—even hundreds—of Web sites, source documents, and photos related to your report topic.

Please see "To Our Readers" on the Copyright page for important information about this book, the MyReportLinks.com Books Web site, and the Report Links that back up this book.

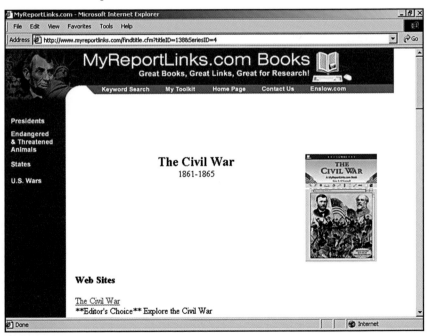

Access:

The Publisher will provide access to the Report Links that back up this book and will try to keep these Report Links up to date on our Web site for three years from the book's first publication date. Please enter **ACW2535** if asked for a password.

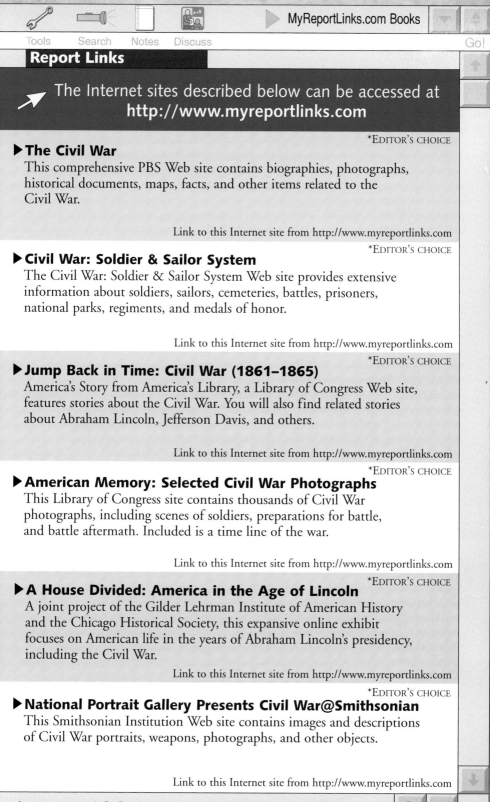

Report Links

The Internet sites described below can be accessed at
http://www.myreportlinks.com

*EDITOR'S CHOICE

▶ **The Civil War**
This comprehensive PBS Web site contains biographies, photographs, historical documents, maps, facts, and other items related to the Civil War.

Link to this Internet site from http://www.myreportlinks.com

*EDITOR'S CHOICE

▶ **Civil War: Soldier & Sailor System**
The Civil War: Soldier & Sailor System Web site provides extensive information about soldiers, sailors, cemeteries, battles, prisoners, national parks, regiments, and medals of honor.

Link to this Internet site from http://www.myreportlinks.com

*EDITOR'S CHOICE

▶ **Jump Back in Time: Civil War (1861–1865)**
America's Story from America's Library, a Library of Congress Web site, features stories about the Civil War. You will also find related stories about Abraham Lincoln, Jefferson Davis, and others.

Link to this Internet site from http://www.myreportlinks.com

*EDITOR'S CHOICE

▶ **American Memory: Selected Civil War Photographs**
This Library of Congress site contains thousands of Civil War photographs, including scenes of soldiers, preparations for battle, and battle aftermath. Included is a time line of the war.

Link to this Internet site from http://www.myreportlinks.com

*EDITOR'S CHOICE

▶ **A House Divided: America in the Age of Lincoln**
A joint project of the Gilder Lehrman Institute of American History and the Chicago Historical Society, this expansive online exhibit focuses on American life in the years of Abraham Lincoln's presidency, including the Civil War.

Link to this Internet site from http://www.myreportlinks.com

*EDITOR'S CHOICE

▶ **National Portrait Gallery Presents Civil War@Smithsonian**
This Smithsonian Institution Web site contains images and descriptions of Civil War portraits, weapons, photographs, and other objects.

Link to this Internet site from http://www.myreportlinks.com

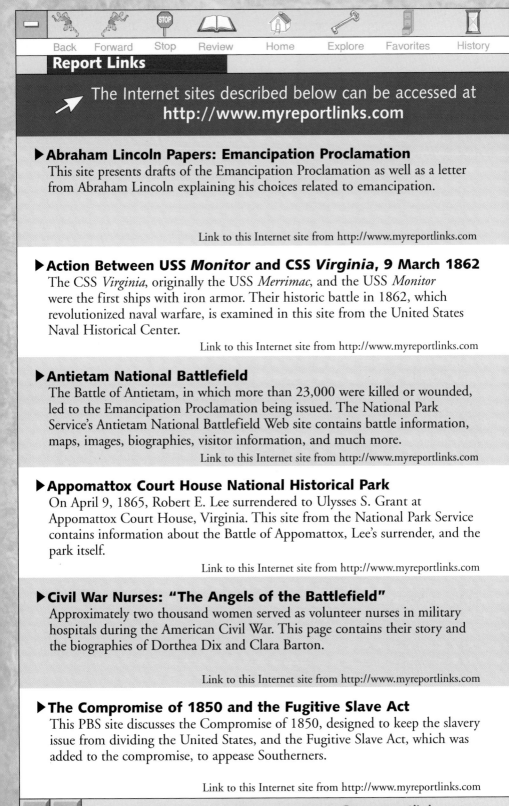

The Internet sites described below can be accessed at
http://www.myreportlinks.com

▶**Abraham Lincoln Papers: Emancipation Proclamation**
This site presents drafts of the Emancipation Proclamation as well as a letter
from Abraham Lincoln explaining his choices related to emancipation.

Link to this Internet site from http://www.myreportlinks.com

▶**Action Between USS *Monitor* and CSS *Virginia*, 9 March 1862**
The CSS *Virginia*, originally the USS *Merrimac*, and the USS *Monitor*
were the first ships with iron armor. Their historic battle in 1862, which
revolutionized naval warfare, is examined in this site from the United States
Naval Historical Center.

Link to this Internet site from http://www.myreportlinks.com

▶**Antietam National Battlefield**
The Battle of Antietam, in which more than 23,000 were killed or wounded,
led to the Emancipation Proclamation being issued. The National Park
Service's Antietam National Battlefield Web site contains battle information,
maps, images, biographies, visitor information, and much more.

Link to this Internet site from http://www.myreportlinks.com

▶**Appomattox Court House National Historical Park**
On April 9, 1865, Robert E. Lee surrendered to Ulysses S. Grant at
Appomattox Court House, Virginia. This site from the National Park Service
contains information about the Battle of Appomattox, Lee's surrender, and the
park itself.

Link to this Internet site from http://www.myreportlinks.com

▶**Civil War Nurses: "The Angels of the Battlefield"**
Approximately two thousand women served as volunteer nurses in military
hospitals during the American Civil War. This page contains their story and
the biographies of Dorthea Dix and Clara Barton.

Link to this Internet site from http://www.myreportlinks.com

▶**The Compromise of 1850 and the Fugitive Slave Act**
This PBS site discusses the Compromise of 1850, designed to keep the slavery
issue from dividing the United States, and the Fugitive Slave Act, which was
added to the compromise, to appease Southerners.

Link to this Internet site from http://www.myreportlinks.com

▶ **Crisis at Fort Sumter**
The first event of the war is examined in this site from Tulane
University. A variety of resources focus not only on the crisis of
Fort Sumter, but also the causes and effects of the conflict.

Link to this Internet site from http://www.myreportlinks.com

▶ **The Dred Scott Case**
Dred Scott, a slave, failed to win his freedom through the United States
legal system. The Supreme Court ruled that as a slave he was property
and not a citizen. This Web site from Washington University Libraries
contains documentation on the Dred Scott case.

Link to this Internet site from http://www.myreportlinks.com

▶ **Fifty-fourth Massachusetts Infantry**
The Fifty-fourth Massachusetts was an African-American infantry unit
that fought valiantly at Fort Wagner, South Carolina. Here you will
find their story, photographs, and other information about black
soldiers in the Civil War.

Link to this Internet site from http://www.myreportlinks.com

▶ **The Frederick Douglass Papers**
Frederick Douglass was an escaped slave, abolitionist, editor, orator,
and public servant. This Library of Congress site contains the electronic
texts of Douglass's papers, including a draft of his autobiography and
his speeches.

Link to this Internet site from http://www.myreportlinks.com

▶ **Fredericksburg and Spotsylvania National Military Park**
This National Park Service site contains information about the Battle
of Fredericksburg, the Battle of Chancellorsville, the Battle of the
Wilderness, the Battle of Spotsylvania, and the Battle of Todd's Tavern.
Visitor information, maps, links, and other resources are included.

Link to this Internet site from http://www.myreportlinks.com

▶ **The Gettysburg Address**
This Library of Congress Web site contains Lincoln's two drafts of the
Gettysburg Address, translations of the document, Lincoln's invitation
to speak at Gettysburg, and the only known photograph of Lincoln
at Gettysburg.

Link to this Internet site from http://www.myreportlinks.com

Report Links

➤ The Internet sites described below can be accessed at
http://www.myreportlinks.com

▶ **John Brown's Holy War**

This multimedia site from PBS contains the story of John Brown and the Harpers Ferry raid. Here you will find interactive maps, videos, primary sources, biographies, interview transcripts, a time line, and other resources that illustrate the story.

Link to this Internet site from http://www.myreportlinks.com

▶ **Manassas**

Manassas National Battlefield Park was the site of the two Battles at Manassas, also called Bull Run. The National Park Service's Web site contains battle information, virtual tours of the park, visitor information, and more.

Link to this Internet site from http://www.myreportlinks.com

▶ **Notre Dame Archives—William Tecumseh Sherman Family Papers**

General William T. Sherman fought in the Civil War and the Indian Wars. This site from the Notre Dame Archives contains his biography, diaries, correspondence, and other resources.

Link to this Internet site from http://www.myreportlinks.com

▶ **The Papers of Jefferson Davis**

This comprehensive site from Rice University contains the papers of Jefferson Davis, the president of the Confederate States of America, as well as information about him.

Link to this Internet site from http://www.myreportlinks.com

▶ **Stonewall Jackson Resources: VMI Archives**

One of the most important Confederate generals was Thomas J. "Stonewall" Jackson. This site from the Virginia Military Institute, where Jackson once taught, contains biographical information, the complete text of Jackson's letters, and other resources.

Link to this Internet site from http://www.myreportlinks.com

▶ **The Time of the Lincolns**

This wide-ranging PBS site is dedicated to American life during the time of Abraham and Mary Lincoln. The topics covered include partisan politics, newspapers, slavery, abolitionists, the Civil War, war photography, women's rights, medical care, and the lives of ordinary people.

Link to this Internet site from http://www.myreportlinks.com

Any comments? Contact us: **comments@myreportlinks.com**

Report Links

The Internet sites described below can be accessed at
http://www.myreportlinks.com

▶**Ulysses S. Grant**
This interactive PBS Web site contains a wealth of information about
Ulysses S. Grant. Here you will find biographies, descriptions of events,
an image gallery, a time line, and the text of Grant's memoirs.

Link to this Internet site from http://www.myreportlinks.com

▶***Uncle Tom's Cabin* and American Culture:
A Multimedia Archive**
Harriet Beecher Stowe's antislavery novel *Uncle Tom's Cabin* and its
role in American culture are explored in this site. Included are reviews,
pro-slavery responses, African-American responses, songs, and more.

Link to this Internet site from http://www.myreportlinks.com

▶**United States Civil War Center**
This United States Civil War Center is dedicated to the study of the
Civil War from different perspectives and disciplines. Here you will
find online exhibits, information about how to begin research, and
links to other Civil War resources online.

Link to this Internet site from http://www.myreportlinks.com

▶**The Valley of the Shadow: Two Communities
During the Civil War**
This Web site follows two Northern and Southern communities
through the events of the Civil War. Here you will find thousands of
sources that help paint a picture of what life was like on the home front.

Link to this Internet site from http://www.myreportlinks.com

▶**Vicksburg National Military Park**
The Campaign for Vicksburg was important in opening up the
Mississippi River for the Union. The National Park Service Web site for
Vicksburg National Military Park contains the story of the campaign,
siege, and surrender. Photos, maps, and visitor information are included.

Link to this Internet site from http://www.myreportlinks.com

▶**Wikipedia: Robert E. Lee**
West Point superintendent, Mexican War veteran, and hero of Harpers
Ferry, Robert E. Lee declined Abraham Lincoln's invitation to command
the United States army during the Civil War. Lee instead became the
Confederacy's leading general. This site offers a biography of Lee.

Link to this Internet site from http://www.myreportlinks.com

Civil War Facts

▷ **Casualties** About 623,000 lost in battle or to disease and injury: 360,000 Union and 260,000 Confederate. Approximately 471,000 wounded*

▷ **Combatants** The United States of America; The Confederate States of America

▷ **Number of Battlefields** Approximately 10,000

These casualty figures include deaths from battle, from injury, from disease, and during imprisonment. All figures are approximate and reflect the majority of scholarly sources.

▷ **Timeline of Major Battles, 1861–1865**

July 21, 1861—First Battle of Manassas/Bull Run, Manassas, Va.; Union army is defeated and first realizes the seriousness of the war.

Feb. 6, 1862—Fort Henry, Tenn.; First Union victory.

June 25–July 1, 1862—Seven Days battles, outside Richmond, Va.; Union army retreats, and Richmond stays in Confederate hands.

Aug. 27–30, 1862—Second Battle of Manassas/Bull Run, Manassas, Va.; The Confederacy regains almost all of Virginia.

Sept. 17, 1862—Antietam, Sharpsburg, Md.; Bloodiest single day of fighting in American history, and strategic victory for Union army.

Dec. 13, 1862—Fredericksburg, Va.; Overwhelming Confederate victory leaves the Union army demoralized and with more than 12,000 dead.

May 1–4, 1863—Chancellorsville, Va.; Another Confederate victory, but one tempered by the loss of Stonewall Jackson.

May 19–July 4, 1863—Siege of Vicksburg, Miss.; Union victory allows North to control Mississippi River and the West.

July 1–3, 1863—Gettysburg, Pa.; Union victory marks a turning point in the war.

Sept. 19–20, 1863—Chickamauga, Ga.; Brutal battle considered a Confederate victory.

Nov. 23–25, 1863—Chattanooga, Tenn.; Union win results in most of Tennessee in Northern hands.

May 5–19, 1864—Spotsylvania and the Wilderness battles, Va.; No clear-cut winner, but heavy losses on both sides.

June 1–3, 1864—Cold Harbor, outside Richmond, Va.; Lee's last major victory.

June 20, 1864–April 2, 1865—Siege of Petersburg, Va.; Trench warfare lasting nine months keeps Confederate army on the defensive and without supplies.

A Fateful Charge

The field before them seemed to shimmer in the steamy July heat. Tired, dirty, and thirsty, the Confederate army lined up along a low ridge near Gettysburg, Pennsylvania, waiting for the next command. The soldiers had already seen two days of fierce fighting on the nearby rocky hills and meadows. They took whatever rest they could, turning their rifles into leaning posts. Across the open field, they could see the Union army behind a stone wall on higher ground. As the Union commanders finished lunch, the Confederate army unleashed its cannons, interrupting the meal with exploding shells.

Union general Winfield Scott Hancock was among those in command. The cannon fire threatened to scatter the Union soldiers, so Hancock rode his horse along the line to encourage his troops. When someone warned him not to risk his life, Hancock answered, "There are times when a corps commander's life does

Major General Winfield Scott ▶ Hancock, a Pennsylvania native and West Point graduate, was considered one of the Union army's best corps commanders. At Gettysburg, he was wounded during the battle by a nail and by wood fragments, possibly from his saddle being driven into his thigh.

The Civil War . The War . Biographies of Key Figures . Longstreet | PBS - Microsoft Internet Explorer

File Edit View Favorites Tools Help

Links »

Address http://www.pbs.org/civilwar/war/biographies/longstreet.html

THE
CIVIL WAR
A FILM BY KEN BURNS

IMAGES OF THE CIVIL WAR

THE FILM, PAST AND PRESENT

THE WAR
Maps
Biographies ►
Historical Documents
Bibliography
Related Links
Fact Page

THE FILMMAKERS

IN THE CLASSROOM

SCREENSAVER

Prev | Next

Clara Barton

Pierre Gustave
Toutant Beauregard

Mary Ann Bickerdyke

John Wilkes Booth

Mathew Brady

John Brown

Ambrose Burnside

John Caldwell
Calhoun

Joshua Lawrence
Chamberlain

Mary Boykin
Chestnut

Jefferson Davis

Dorothea Lynde Dix

Frederick Douglass

David Farragut

Nathan Bedford
Forrest

U. S. Grant

BIOGRAPHY:
JAMES LONGSTREET

South

1821-1904

South Carolina

General

James Longstreet's hesitancy and differences of opinion with Robert E. Lee have often marred his historical image. Although generally respected for his military prowess, he is often blamed for the Confederate defeat at Gettysburg for allowing Pickett's charge to occur. Yet Longstreet remained a prominent national figure after the war. In 1880, the West Point graduate and prosperous businessman was named U.S. minister to Turkey.

Document: Done

Internet

▲ Another West Point graduate, Confederate general James Longstreet opposed Robert E. Lee's decision to have his forces attack at Gettysburg.

not count."[1] The Union army responded with its own volley of artillery fire.

Yet the guns eventually fell silent. The Union commanders, who believed that a charge was coming, wanted to lure the Confederate army out of the woods. The strategy worked. General James Longstreet's First Corps of 15,000 men began to advance, shoulder to shoulder, away from the tree line. The steel of their bayonets shone in the hot sun, visible to the Union line. The Union cannons opened up again, mowing down the advancing Confederate soldiers in shocking numbers.

Still the Southern army kept coming. Confederate general Lewis Armistead rushed ahead of the line, urging his men onward. Armistead and Hancock had been good friends before the war, but friendship could not keep them from choosing opposite sides.

To stay visible and encourage his men, Armistead took off his hat and stabbed it onto the end of his sword. With Armistead waving his sword like a flag, his soldiers finally reached the Union line. There, many men were killed at close range, and Armistead was among those mortally wounded. But even war could not kill friendship. Armistead's last words included a request that Hancock, rather than a member of his own army, send his personal items home to his family.

This ill-fated charge has become known as Pickett's Charge, named for one of its leaders, the colorful Confederate general George Pickett. The Confederate army had tried, and failed, to push into Union territory, to move the war out of the South and threaten the nation's capital. Up to that point, the Confederates had won many decisive battles, and they felt that total victory was within their reach. But after the Battle of Gettysburg, the Southern armies were never able to push into Union territory again.

In four bloody years, the American Civil War was fought in 10,000 places, from as far north as Pennsylvania to as far south as Florida and as far west as New Mexico. The war brought death and poverty to many families, both North and South. But as was the case with Armistead and Hancock, the Civil War also proved the ability of Americans to heal their wounds and mend fences with their enemies. Fought over slavery, states' rights, and the authority of the federal government, the American Civil War changed the face of America forever.

The Coming Storm

The causes of the American Civil War have been debated for more than a century. Most historians agree that the sectional differences between North and South were one factor. The North, with a larger population, had much more industry than the South. The North was thus becoming modernized more quickly, and its economy depended on trade rather than agriculture. The South, with fewer people, was still primarily rural in the mid-nineteenth century. It was the home of cotton and tobacco and an economy based on slave labor.

Historians also agree that the battle over states' rights, with the South supporting the rights of individual states over the power of the federal government, was another factor that led Southern states to secede from, or leave, the Union. But every difference between North and South eventually involved the question of slavery.

▶ The Peculiar Institution

Virginia, known as the mother of presidents, might also be called the mother of slavery. The colony that produced our nation's earliest supporters of freedom and independence, including George Washington and Thomas Jefferson, is also where the "peculiar institution" of slavery, as Southerners referred to it, first took hold.

Africans were brought to the Jamestown settlement in 1619 as indentured servants—they were promised freedom after a certain period of time. But over the next century, the colonies established laws making African

Americans and their offspring slaves for life. Slavery was profitable for the colonies, ensuring workers to produce bounty in the fields, and it also provided jobs in the slave trade. The colonies worked to keep it that way. In 1705, the Virginia General Assembly stated that if slaves resisted their masters, and were killed as a result, the master "shall be free of all punishment."[1]

The practice of slavery was as cruel to the black men and women who were slaves as it was profitable for slaveholders. Slaves were deprived of even the most basic pleasures such as knowing and being able to celebrate their birthdays. "A want of information concerning my

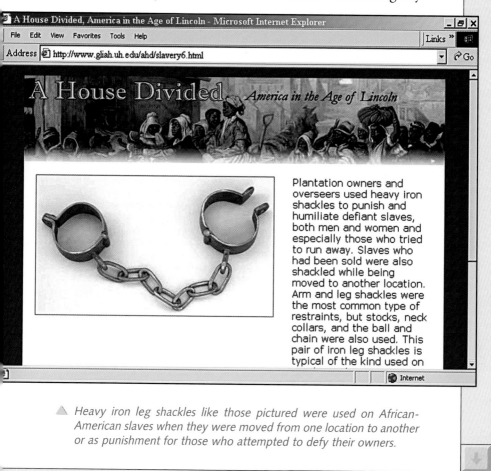

A House Divided, America in the Age of Lincoln - Microsoft Internet Explorer

File   Edit   View   Favorites   Tools   Help   Links »

Address http://www.gliah.uh.edu/ahd/slavery6.html   Go

A House Divided *America in the Age of Lincoln*

Plantation owners and overseers used heavy iron shackles to punish and humiliate defiant slaves, both men and women and especially those who tried to run away. Slaves who had been sold were also shackled while being moved to another location. Arm and leg shackles were the most common type of restraints, but stocks, neck collars, and the ball and chain were also used. This pair of iron leg shackles is typical of the kind used on

Heavy iron leg shackles like those pictured were used on African-American slaves when they were moved from one location to another or as punishment for those who attempted to defy their owners.

own [birthday] was a source of unhappiness to me even during childhood," wrote Frederick Douglass, a famous African-American orator and former slave. "The white children could tell their ages. I could not tell why I ought to be deprived of the same privilege."[2]

Calling for Abolition

By 1820 the great westward expansion of the United States had begun, and soon the question was raised whether slavery should continue in the new territories. That year the Missouri Compromise allowed the addition of Missouri, a slave state, to the Union, as the nation was often called then. To maintain a balance between the states that allowed slavery and those that did not, Maine was admitted as a free state, and slavery was prohibited in those territories obtained in the Louisiana Purchase that lay above a certain line of latitude. But slavery continued to divide North and South, as Northern abolitionists sought to end the practice, and Southern slaveholders sought to preserve their way of life.

The Compromise of 1850 and the Fugitive Slave Act

A group of acts passed by Congress in 1850 tried to keep

Orator, abolitionist, statesman, and author, Frederick Douglass began life as a slave in Maryland. He became the first African American to hold a high-ranking position in U.S. government, as the United States minister and consul general to Haiti.

the question of slavery from tearing the country apart. With the Compromise of 1850, the slave trade was banned from Washington, D.C., but slavery could continue elsewhere, and in new territories, the decision to permit slavery would be left up to the white citizens of those territories. Attached to the Compromise was the Fugitive Slave Law, which required Northerners to return slaves seeking freedom to their owners. That law angered abolitionists, who established the Underground Railroad—not an actual railroad but a system or network of safe houses that led slaves to free lands in the North as well as Canada and Mexico. And in 1852, Harriet Beecher Stowe published *Uncle Tom's Cabin,* a novel about the hardships of a brave and good-hearted slave, which was an attack on the Fugitive Slave Law. Within a year, more than 300,000 copies were sold.

▶ The Kansas-Nebraska Act and the Dred Scott Decision

Efforts were just as strong to keep slavery firmly in place, however. In 1854, the Kansas-Nebraska Act allowed white citizens of those territories to decide whether to permit slavery there by popular vote, a process known as popular sovereignty. Fighting in Kansas between abolitionists and slaveholding settlers led to more than two hundred deaths. Three years later, in the Dred Scott case, the U.S. Supreme Court ruled that the Missouri Compromise was unconstitutional. Dred Scott was a Missouri slave who had sued his owner in 1846 for freedom on the grounds that Scott's owner had taken him into Illinois, a free state, and into the Wisconsin Territory, which by the terms of the Missouri Compromise banned slavery. The Court ruled that Scott was neither a citizen of Missouri nor the

United States and that his stay in a free territory did not make him free. It further ruled that Congress could not bar slavery from a territory, as it had done in the Missouri Compromise. The Dred Scott decision led to the expansion of slavery into the territories—and deepened the divide between North and South. At the time, the United States was home to about 4 million slaves.

▶ John Brown's Raid

In 1859, John Brown, an uncommon man with a common name, led the nation closer to war. Brown was an outspoken abolitionist who thought that slavery would never end without a fight. With a band of men, he launched an attack on a Union weapons storehouse in Harpers Ferry, Virginia (now West Virginia), with the aim of arming slaves and winning support for abolition. The attack failed, and Brown was injured and captured by a group of U.S. Marines. One of their commanders was a lifelong soldier named Robert E. Lee. Brown was executed for his crime, making abolitionists even angrier.

▶ A House Divided

The following year, 1860, as North and South moved further apart on the slavery issue, a lawyer from Illinois—Abraham Lincoln—was elected president. Lincoln had promised to keep slavery from spreading into new states and territories where it did not already exist. The tall and awkward Lincoln was not popular in the slaveholding states, where his name had not even appeared on the ballot. Southern states had threatened to secede from the Union if Lincoln were elected. In 1858, in his acceptance speech after being nominated the Republican candidate for the U.S. Senate from Illinois, Lincoln realized that

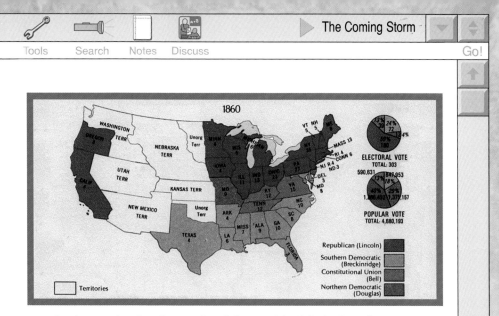

1860

ELECTORAL VOTE
TOTAL: 303

POPULAR VOTE
TOTAL: 4,680,193

Republican (Lincoln)
Southern Democratic (Breckinridge)
Constitutional Union (Bell)
Northern Democratic (Douglas)

Territories

▲ *A map showing the results of the presidential election of 1860 in which Abraham Lincoln was elected president.*

slavery threatened the very preservation of the Union when he quoted these words from the Bible: "A house divided against itself cannot stand."[3]

▶ Secession

In December 1860, South Carolina made good on its threat and seceded from the Union. Several states followed. In February 1861, a convention of seceded states, including South Carolina, Mississippi, Florida, Alabama, Georgia, Louisiana, and Texas, adopted the first constitution of the Confederate States of America. They elected a former senator from Mississippi named Jefferson Davis as the president of the Confederacy. Arkansas, Tennessee, Virginia, and North Carolina followed these states into the Confederacy in a matter of months. Montgomery, Alabama, was the original capital of the Confederate States of America, but in May 1861 the capital was moved to Richmond, Virginia.

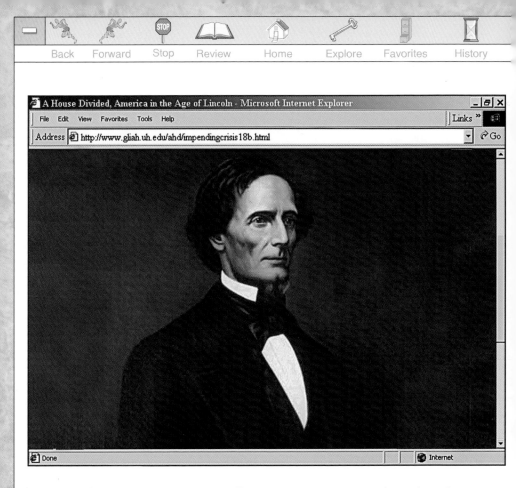

A House Divided, America in the Age of Lincoln - Microsoft Internet Explorer

File Edit View Favorites Tools Help   Links »

Address http://www.gliah.uh.edu/ahd/impendingcrisis18b.html   Go

Done   Internet

▲ *On February 18, 1861, Jefferson Davis was inaugurated president of the Confederate States of America. Like Abraham Lincoln, Davis was born in Kentucky. But unlike him, Davis was a staunch supporter of slavery. A military veteran of the Black Hawk War and the Mexican-American War, Davis had hoped to receive a military post with the Confederacy.*

▷ The Call to Arms

Seven states had left the Union by March 4, 1861, when Abraham Lincoln was inaugurated the sixteenth president of the United States. In his first inaugural address, Lincoln made a last plea for peace. "We are not enemies but friends," he said. "We must not be enemies. Though passion may have strained, it must not break our bonds of affection."[4]

The First Shots

Just over a month later, South Carolina broke those bonds. In the darkness before dawn on April 12, 1861, Confederate troops fired the first shots of the war, attacking Union forces at Fort Sumter, in Charleston Harbor. When South Carolina seceded, it demanded all federal property in the state, which included Fort Sumter. When the commander of the fort refused to surrender to a Confederate general, the opening shots of the war rang out. After a day and a half of cannon fire, the Union troops surrendered. Remarkably, a horse suffered the only loss of life.

Almost immediately, Lincoln issued a call for troops to fight the Confederates. Veteran soldiers of the U.S. Army, many who had studied together at the United States Military Academy or served together in the Mexican-American War, would eventually choose sides. Those soldiers who stayed with the Union included Ulysses S. Grant, William Tecumseh Sherman, George B. McClellan, Ambrose Burnside, George G. Meade, and Joshua L. Chamberlain.

Men who decided to fight for the Confederacy included Thomas J. "Stonewall" Jackson, James Longstreet, Albert Sidney Johnston, A. P. Hill, and Joseph E. Johnston. The decision to leave the U.S. Army was a painful one for Robert E. Lee, a past superintendent of the United States Military Academy, a decorated soldier, and an opponent of secession. He refused Abraham Lincoln's offer to command the Union army and resigned his commission April 20, 1861—the day that Virginia, his home state, seceded. Although Lee would become the South's leading general, he called secession "the beginning of sorrows."[5]

War Erupts, 1861–1862

In the summer of 1861, many citizens were working to support the war effort. Wilmer McLean, who owned a farm near Manassas, Virginia, allowed his house to be used as a Confederate headquarters. He regretted that decision when a Union shell exploded in his living room. The Union and Confederate armies had met on the rolling fields near McLean's farm, along a stream called Bull Run, to fight the first major land battle of the Civil War.

▶ First Battle of Manassas/Bull Run

In June, Union troops had slowly advanced from Washington, D.C., into the Virginia countryside, where Confederate soldiers waited for them at Manassas. When they finally clashed on July 21, soldiers in both armies lacked battle experience and were often confused. Thousands of men were killed and wounded. In the end, the Confederates held their ground, forcing the Union soldiers to retreat. Confederate general Thomas J.

◀ *After Robert E. Lee, Thomas Jonathan "Stonewall" Jackson was the most admired Confederate leader. His victories against overwhelming odds in several battles earned him lasting fame.*

Jackson was among the victors, earning the nickname "Stonewall" because he stood firm before the enemy.

This battle is known as both Manassas and Bull Run. The U.S. Army often named battles after landmarks or waterways, while the Confederacy named them after the closest town. As a result, many battles have more than one name.

In the early days of the war, some people did not take the fighting seriously. Spectators brought picnic baskets and sat on nearby hillsides to watch the fight as if the armies were sports teams—the Yankees, as the Union soldiers in their blue uniforms were called, against the Rebels, the Southern boys in shades of gray. The blood that was shed on both sides, however, soon showed everyone that the war would be long and difficult.

After the battle, Wilmer McLean tried to escape the war by moving south to a town called Appomattox Court House, in Virginia. But the war would find him again, four long years later.

▶ Moving West

The next year found the war expanding into new regions, called "theaters." The main areas in which Civil War battles took place were the eastern theater, including coastal states such as Virginia and the Carolinas; the western theater, the region between the Appalachian Mountains and the Mississippi River; and the Trans-Mississippi Department, which consisted of Arkansas, Texas, Missouri, Indian Territory, and parts of Louisiana west of the Mississippi.

In February 1862, both armies were focused on the western theater, especially the Cumberland and Tennessee Rivers, which cut through Tennessee. If an army controlled key places along important rivers, it was harder for

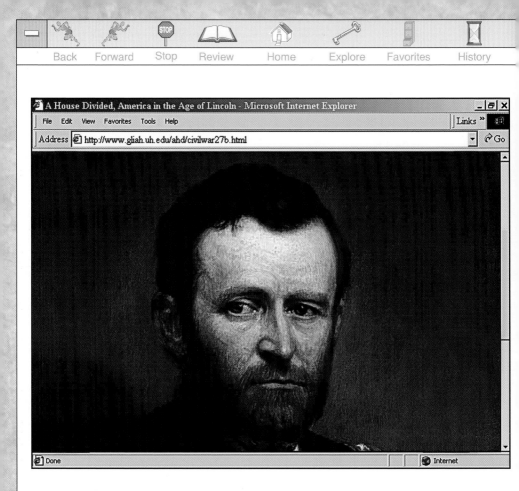

A House Divided, America in the Age of Lincoln - Microsoft Internet Explorer

File   Edit   View   Favorites   Tools   Help   Links »

Address   http://www.gliah.uh.edu/ahd/civilwar27b.html   Go

Done   Internet

▲ *Ulysses S. Grant entered the Civil War a poor man, having achieved little in his life. After Grant led his men to victories in the West during 1862 and 1863, President Lincoln appointed him general-in-chief of the Union armies.*

the enemy to move troops and supplies. So armies often fought again and again to control central waterways.

Years before the Civil War, Ulysses S. Grant had been forced to resign from the U.S. Army for disorderly behavior. He had rejoined the army in 1861 and was anxious to prove himself. Now a Union general, commanding the Army of the Tennessee, Grant set his sights on Fort Henry, a Confederate fort guarding the Tennessee River. On February 6, Union gunboats bombarded the fort. Although they responded with heavy cannon fire, the rebel troops surrendered before Grant's foot soldiers even arrived. It was the first important victory for the Union army.

On February 12, Grant then moved his forces toward Fort Donelson, on the Cumberland River, where the Confederate soldiers staged a brutal attack. By February 16, however, more than 12,000 Confederate soldiers surrendered. Newspaper accounts soon said that Grant's initials, U. S., stood for "Unconditional Surrender."

The Battle of Shiloh

Confident in his victories, Grant had moved his army by early April along the Tennessee River toward a town called Pittsburg Landing. There, soldiers pitched their tents near the small Shiloh Church and rested for the night. They were rudely awakened early on April 6 by screaming rebels and gunfire. Confederate general Albert Sidney Johnston had launched a surprise attack.

On the battle's first day, thousands of Union soldiers were killed, and others ran for their lives, although later that day some Yankees had reformed a battle line along a sunken road they called "the Hornet's Nest." By day's end, however, the survivors were forced to surrender. But this had given Grant enough time to strengthen his army's position elsewhere. His trusted friend and fellow general William Tecumseh Sherman saw Grant resting and asked, "We've had the devil's own day, haven't we?"

"Yes," Grant said, not beaten yet. "[We'll] lick 'em tomorrow."[1]

The next morning, April 7, Grant's army attacked, after receiving reinforcements overnight from the Army of the Ohio under the command of General Don Carlos Buell. After a day of fighting, Confederate general Johnston was killed, and the Confederate army retreated.

Although Grant had won again, victory came at a heavy price. In just two days, the Battle of Shiloh had killed or wounded more than 13,000 Union soldiers and more than 10,000 Confederate soldiers.

Back in Virginia

As soldiers fought over rivers in the West, the armies faced each other on land and at sea in the East. In March 1862, a new age of naval warfare began with the battle at Hampton Roads, Virginia, of the ironclad ships the USS *Monitor* and the *Merrimac*. (The Confederate army renamed the USS *Merrimac* the CSS *Virginia* after capturing the naval yard at

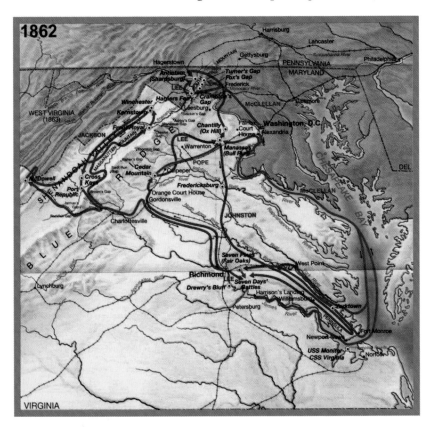

▲ The war in 1862.

Norfolk and raising the ship.) The *Monitor's* design was new; the *Merrimac* was a wooden ship covered with iron plating that resisted enemy fire. Although the two ships shelled each other for four hours, neither ship could punch a hole through the other. The battle ended with no clear victor. But this famous duel meant that all existing warships without iron sides were immediately outdated.

Stonewall Jackson: Victories in the Shenandoah Valley

On land, in Virginia's Shenandoah Valley, Confederate general Stonewall Jackson was making a name for himself as well. Jackson was deeply religious and somewhat strange, sucking on lemons even during battles. But he was also fearless and demanding, ordering his men to march for twenty-five miles a day. They became known as Jackson's "foot cavalry." In the warming spring of 1862, Jackson's soldiers won a string of victories throughout the Shenandoah Valley, which was vital farm country for the Confederacy.

Jackson became Lee's most trusted officer. "Such an executive officer the sun never shone on," Lee said later. "I have but to show him my design, and I know that if it can be done, it will be done."[2]

By summer 1862, the Seven Days battles near Richmond forced the retreat of Union general George McClellan and kept the Confederate capital from falling into Union hands. In August a second battle near Manassas resulted in yet another Confederate victory, one in which the South regained nearly all of Virginia. The Second Battle of Manassas or Bull Run was a stunning win for Robert E. Lee, and the South began to feel that the war was going their way.

The Bloodiest Day—Antietam

Although the Confederates had won many key victories, almost all of the battles had taken place on their own soil. Lee was eager to take the fighting north for several reasons: to keep the momentum he had achieved at Manassas, to threaten the nation's capital and thus draw the Union army out of Virginia, and to give Virginia's farmers the peace they needed to gather their harvests—and provide his men with needed supplies for the coming winter. His hungry and worn-out troops left the bloody fields of Virginia and turned toward the untouched farmlands of Maryland instead. The army crossed the Potomac River in mid-September.

Lee met the Union forces, led by McClellan, on a field near Antietam Creek, which curved past the town of Sharpsburg, Maryland. As the sun moved high in the sky on September 17, the armies battered each other again and again—through cornfields, along a sunken road that would be renamed Bloody Lane, and finally across a stone bridge over Antietam Creek. When the sun set, as much blue as gray could be seen lying in the fields. One day of fighting had lost 23,000 men—17,000

General George B. McClellan's failure to pursue Robert E. Lee after the Battle of Antietam and his criticisms of his commander-in-chief, Abraham Lincoln, led him to be relieved of his command in the Union army in 1862. McClellan then entered politics and was elected governor of New Jersey.

wounded and 6,000 dead. The battle of Antietam remains the bloodiest single day in American history.

Suffering terrible losses, Lee had no choice but to retreat south to Virginia. The battle was considered a strategic victory for the Union, although McClellan's failure to pursue Lee led President Lincoln to relieve McClellan of his command two months later.

The Emancipation Proclamation

Encouraged that the Union had held firm at Antietam, and hoping to further hurt the South's ability to wage war, President Lincoln issued a draft of the Emancipation Proclamation on September 22, which declared freedom as of January 1863 for those slaves in the states that were still in rebellion. It did not set all slaves free—the Thirteenth Amendment to the Constitution, ratified on December 6, 1865, after the war, did that. And it could not be enforced—it was a promise of freedom, not an act that ensured it. Though limited in its scope, the proclamation was hailed by abolitionists and caused Great Britain and France to refrain from supporting the Confederacy.

A Hard Winter, 1862–1863

In a year of heavy losses, the coming of winter brought even more hardships. It was particularly hard for the citizens of Fredericksburg, Virginia. In mid-December, expecting a Union attack, the Confederate government had urged Fredericksburg residents to leave their homes for their own safety. Union general Ambrose Burnside planned to lead his men across the nearby Rappahannock River and into attack formation. But it took too many days to build the needed bridges. By the time Burnside's

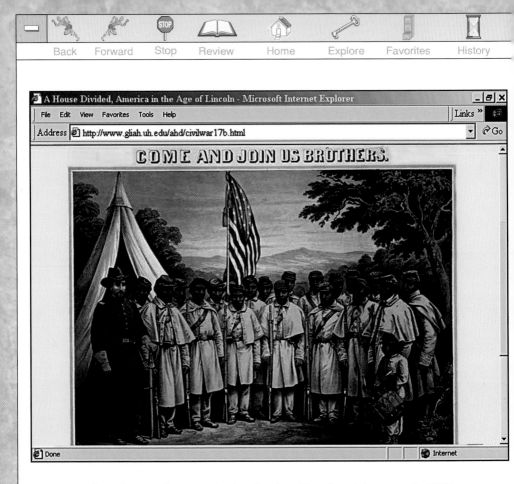

COME AND JOIN US BROTHERS.

Following the Emancipation Proclamation, the Union army in 1863 began recruiting African-American men. This recruiting poster depicts an African-American unit, which was segregated and led by white officers.

soldiers got across, a line of 75,000 rebels stretched along on the high ground overlooking the Rappahannock.

The Battle of Fredericksburg

Burnside's troops focused their attack on a hilly area called Marye's Heights, but the rebels were ready with their cannons. Row upon row of Yankee soldiers were killed before Burnside finally halted the attack. It was a terrible defeat for the Union army, with more than 12,000 casualties. Yet not every rebel celebrated the one-sided victory. A kind

Confederate named Richard Kirkland risked being shot to bring water to wounded Union soldiers. He became known as the "Angel of Marye's Heights."

Forever Free

With the dawn of the new year, the Emancipation Proclamation went into effect. The proclamation changed the character of the war, since the Union army and navy were soon allowed to enlist African-American soldiers and sailors. As he issued the historic proclamation, Lincoln said, "I never, in my life, felt more certain that I was doing right, than I do in signing this paper."[3]

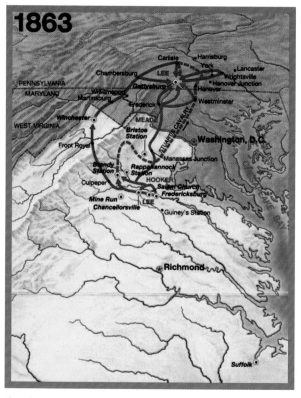

▲ *The war in 1863.*

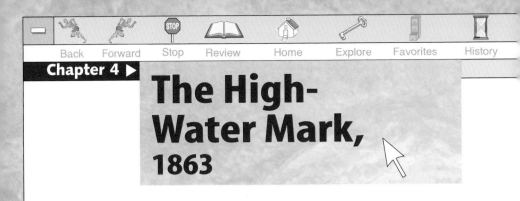

Chapter 4 ▶

The High-Water Mark, 1863

Wintry weather in Virginia gave both armies a break from fighting, and some healthier soldiers passed the time with spirited snowball fights. But most soldiers were busy trying to fight off the disease and hunger common in the winter camps. Hundreds fled the armies and left for home each day.

Spring found President Lincoln searching, once again, for someone to head the Union army. He had been disappointed in George McClellan and Ambrose Burnside, so he decided to give command to Joseph Hooker from Massachusetts, known as "Fighting Joe."

▶ Chancellorsville

In late April, Hooker advanced his Union troops toward Chancellorsville, ten miles west of Fredericksburg, where Lee's army remained. Hooker had far more men and was better supplied than Lee, but he was outmaneuvered by the Confederate general. Rather than continuing to advance, Hooker became spooked by the tangled woods known as the Wilderness. He made the fateful decision to wait for more Union troops, buying the Confederates enough time to divide their troops, move them around, and confuse the Yankees. When the attack came, on May 1, the rebels pushed Hooker's men back a couple of miles. The battle went on for four days, with approximately 17,000 casualties on the Union side and 13,000 on the Confederate side. It was hailed as a great victory for

Robert E. Lee's decision to lead the Confederate army was a painful one for him. Lee was not in favor of dissolving the Union, but his loyalty to Virginia, his home, finally won out when it seceded.

Robert E. Lee and his troops, though it came at a great cost.

To press their lead in the battle, Stonewall Jackson and a few officers had taken a moonlit ride on the second night of the campaign to scout the Union position. But nervous Confederate lookouts mistook Jackson for the enemy, shooting him in the right hand and left arm. He was moved to a field hospital, where his arm was amputated. In a weakened state, he soon caught pneumonia. Lee, who remained hopeful that his most daring general would recover, referred to his dependence on Jackson: "He has lost his left arm, but I have lost my right."[1]

On May 10, Jackson died, and the self-confidence that had led the Confederates to many victories seemed to suffer. Although he felt that no commander could match Jackson's talent, Lee took his army north once again.

Turning Point at Gettysburg

As June gave way to July, the two main armies operating in the eastern theater moved toward Gettysburg, Pennsylvania. Hooker had resigned, and Lincoln put his faith in George Gordon Meade to lead the Union army. Meade was a Pennsylvanian known for his quick temper.

With Jackson dead, Lee had put his faith in Generals James Longstreet, A. P. Hill, and Richard Ewell to lead his army's three corps of soldiers. When they reached Gettysburg, a quiet town of only 2,400 residents, the armies claimed spots on the rhyming ridges—Seminary Ridge and Cemetery Ridge—that ran north to south nearby.

On July 1, the first day of the battle, the Confederates drove the Yanks backward to two hills on the north end of Cemetery Ridge, but did not finish their attack until the following day. This allowed the Union army to place troops all along Cemetery Ridge, ending at a rocky hill called Little Round Top.

When the Confederates awoke the next morning, Union troops were in excellent positions on high ground. As the long day wore on, soldiers fought and died in such places as the Wheat Field and around the large rock formations called Devil's Den.

But the day's most frantic struggle took place on Little Round Top, at the very end of the Union line. Rebels had been trying to move cannons to these rocky heights, which would give them a clear shot to destroy the Union line along Cemetery Ridge. Only a few Union regiments defended the hill, including the

Joshua Chamberlain fought at Antietam, Fredericksburg, Chancellorsville, Gettysburg, Spotsylvania, and Cold Harbor. His actions at Gettysburg led to his being awarded the Medal of Honor.

20th Maine, an inexperienced unit led by Joshua L. Chamberlain, formerly a professor and now a colonel.

Wave after wave of rebels charged up Little Round Top, and the soldiers from Maine began to run out of ammunition. Although other officers urged the men to run, Chamberlain bravely suggested that they affix bayonets to the ends of their rifles and charge down the hill instead. "The effect was surprising; many of the enemy's first line threw down their arms and surrendered," Chamberlain recalled. "An officer fired his pistol at my head with one hand while he handed me his sword with the other."[2] Chamberlain's men held the Union position.

As the battle stretched into its third day, Lee's last chance was to attack the center of the Union line. Under the leadership of George Pickett, for whom the charge would be named, and two other commanders, 15,000 men would cross an open field a mile wide. But Meade and his men were waiting for the coming soldiers with rifles and cannons ready. Fully half the rebels who had charged were now dead, wounded, or captured. Some units were completely destroyed.

With Lee accepting all the blame for their loss, the rebels returned to Virginia. Because Lee could never again threaten the North, the Battle of Gettysburg is often called the "High-Water Mark" of the Confederacy. In three days, more than 51,000 soldiers had been killed and wounded—the most devastating battle of the Civil War.

But for Union supporters, July 4 was a day to celebrate. The day after the Union claimed victory at Gettysburg, Union troops under Ulysses S. Grant forced the Confederate surrender of Vicksburg, a key port on the Mississippi River. The Union controlled the Mississippi for the rest of the war, and embittered Vicksburg citizens would not celebrate Independence Day for eighty-two years.

"Our Day Is Coming Fast"

The summer of 1863 also saw a rise in the enlistment of African-American soldiers (then referred to as "colored") into the Union army. By the end of the war, nearly 200,000 of them had joined the fight. Although they were given lowly tasks, were paid less than white soldiers, and often faced racism, black soldiers were proud of their important role. A private in the 54th Massachusetts Colored Infantry even wrote a song to encourage others to join up:

> So rally, boys, rally, let us never mind the past;
> We had a hard road to travel, but our day is coming fast,
> For God is in the right, and we have no need to fear,—
> The Union must be saved by the colored volunteer.[3]

On July 18, 1863, the 54th Massachusetts, which included two sons of Frederick Douglass, saw battle up close. Directed by their white commander, Robert Gould Shaw, the 54th led a charge against Fort Wagner, part of the defenses of Charleston, South Carolina. Despite heavy fire, most of the 54th made it over the fort's walls, where they fought hand to hand with the rebels. More than half of the regiment, including Shaw, were killed. But the 54th Massachusetts proved the courage of black soldiers and their willingness to die for their country. It became the most famous black regiment of the Civil War.

A New Birth of Freedom

As 1863 drew to a close, the war took an important turn. Although Confederates won a brutal battle at

This photograph of President Abraham Lincoln was taken in 1864, during the third long year of the war.

Chickamauga, Georgia, in September, some of the fire had gone out of their fight. A Union victory at nearby Chattanooga, Tennessee, only two months later damaged Southern spirits even more. That October, Lincoln gave Ulysses Grant, who had won so many battles in the West, command of all Union armies in the field.

In November, President Lincoln attended the dedication of a new national cemetery at Gettysburg. After another speaker gave a two-hour speech, Lincoln followed with a speech of only 274 carefully chosen words. He urged the nation to dedicate itself to ending the Civil War, so that "this nation, under God, shall have a new birth of freedom—and that government of the people, by the people, for the people, shall not perish from the earth."[4]

Lincoln suggested that his words, compared to the actions of the brave soldiers who died at Gettysburg, would not be long remembered. He could not have been more wrong. The Gettysburg Address is one of the greatest speeches in American history.

Chapter 5 ▶

The Armies Dig In, 1864–1865

By 1864, Grant could see that the key to winning the war was to wear down the Confederate army, whose numbers were shrinking. In May, a year after they had met at Chancellorsville, the armies clashed again in the same tangled Virginia woods, which they called the Wilderness. The Battle of the Wilderness ended on May 7. The next day and for the next two weeks, they fought again at nearby Spotsylvania Court House. Both battles had no clear winner, but each time Grant caused more casualties in the rebel army. His goal was to capture the Confederate capital at Richmond, not far away.

▲ *The war in 1864.*

General Grant at Cold Harbor, 1864. ▷

A Costly Cold Harbor

In June, Richmond saw one of the war's shortest fights, but also one of the deadliest. By this time, the Confederates had begun to dig trenches and build earthworks to protect themselves from attack. Miles of trench lines zigzagged around Richmond, including a junction called Cold Harbor. There, the rebels had only 59,000 men to face 109,000 attacking Union troops. But the trenches kept the rebels well protected. Union soldiers knew the attack would be costly. Hundreds pinned notes to their uniforms with their names and addresses, so they could be identified if they were killed. In only half an hour, many were. The Union army suffered more than 7,000 casualties. This would be Lee's last major victory.

Marching to the Sea

While the armies dug trenches in Virginia, Union general William Tecumseh Sherman began a slow advance southward from Chattanooga, Tennessee, to Atlanta, Georgia, the heart of the Deep South. He engaged in a sort of military chess game with Confederate general Joseph Johnston in which their two armies clashed, with Johnston retreating more than once as Sherman's forces edged toward Atlanta. Johnston was replaced by John Bell Hood by the

time that Union troops finally invaded Atlanta in early September, destroying miles of railroad track. As citizens fled, Sherman ordered the city burned.

Then, Sherman began his famous "march to the sea." His brutal plan was to march through Georgia to the coastal city of Savannah, destroying as much Confederate property as he could on the way. His campaign cut the South in half and signaled a shift in how the war was waged. Thousands of slaves followed the Union troops, knowing that they would lead the way to freedom. In December, Sherman's men captured Savannah, which he said was his "Christmas gift" to President Lincoln.

Digging In: Petersburg

After they reached the sea, Sherman moved his soldiers north to join the Union armies pounding Petersburg, just south of Richmond. There, the Union army settled in for what would become a ten-month siege, beginning in June and lasting until the end of the war. Their aim was to cut off the Confederate supply lines, forcing the South to surrender or starve. The siege was notable for the continued and widespread use of trench warfare.

Lincoln's Reelection

In November 1864, Abraham Lincoln was reelected president, and the Civil War was in its third year. In his second inaugural address, Lincoln urged the nation

Sherman's victories in the South helped Abraham Lincoln to be reelected in 1864.

to work to "achieve and cherish a just and a lasting peace among ourselves, and with all nations."[1]

▶ The End at Appomattox

Early in April 1865, after another cold winter and months of siege warfare, the hungry and exhausted rebels finally left Richmond and Petersburg in Union control. The Union army blocked the escape of the remaining Confederates at Appomattox Court House, a country village in south-central Virginia. Wanting no more unnecessary killing, Grant sent Lee a respectful request that he surrender. At first, Lee refused.

But after a brief battle in Appomattox killed and wounded more men, Lee knew that his battered army had finally lost. "There is nothing left me to do but to go and see General Grant," he said, "and I would rather die a thousand deaths."[2]

Lee and Grant exchanged messages and agreed to meet in a nearby home on April 9. The chosen house happened to belong to Wilmer McLean, who had moved from Manassas to Appomattox to escape the fighting. The war had begun in his front yard, and now the war was ending in his parlor.

Lee was in his finest dress uniform, adorned with his best sword and a red sash. In contrast, Grant wore his worn blue battle uniform, splattered with mud. The two generals talked about meeting each other years before, when they served together in the Mexican-American War. Their talk soon turned to the terms of surrender. Grant's terms were gracious. He allowed Confederate officers to keep their pistols, and soldiers who owned horses could take them home. Grant and Lee exchanged a few more polite words, and then parted.

Before he left, Lee met Ely Parker, Grant's military secretary, who was a Seneca Indian. "I am glad to see one

▲ *The scene of surrender: the McLean house in Appomattox Court House.*

real American here," Lee said. Parker replied, "We are all Americans."[3]

Soon after, all the remaining rebel armies in the field surrendered too. The war was finally over.

▷ A Celebration Cut Short

With Lee's surrender, joyous citizens throughout the North poured into the streets, laughing and shouting. But the Union could not celebrate long. A week later, on April 14, an actor named John Wilkes Booth shot President Lincoln in the head while Lincoln watched a play at Ford's Theatre in Washington. Booth, who had sympathized with the Confederate cause, leapt to the stage and ran off before the stunned audience could stop him.

Although Lincoln held on to life throughout the night, the president died on the morning of April 15. Standing over the bed with tears in his eyes, Lincoln's secretary of war, Edwin Stanton, raised his arm in salute.

"Now," Stanton said, "he belongs to the ages."[4]

A Lasting Peace

On April 21, a funeral train began the long journey from Washington, D.C., to Springfield, Illinois, carrying Abraham Lincoln's body to its final resting place. John Wilkes Booth was eventually cornered and killed by Union troops. After Confederate soldiers returned home, the South worked to rebuild its destroyed towns and countryside. Families mourned their losses. More than 620,000 soldiers had died in battle or from disease or injury. More Americans were killed in the Civil War than in all other wars combined up to and including the Korean War.

As the government began to rebuild the nation in a period called Reconstruction, Union armies planned a victory parade in Washington, D.C. The new president, Andrew Johnson, stood with Ulysses Grant as 150,000 Union soldiers marched down Pennsylvania Avenue toward the Capitol. American flags hung above them, embroidered with the names of battles that had been so hard fought—Shiloh, Antietam, Gettysburg, Petersburg.

▶ A Nation Changed

The Civil War is sometimes considered the first modern war for its advances in military tactics and in medicine. For example, the war spurred the construction of large hospitals and improved sanitary conditions. It saw the first widespread use of anesthesia (the practice of using medicine to remove pain during surgery) and ambulances. It was also the first war in which photographers followed troops onto the battlefield. The prewar dependence on agriculture in the South gave way to a rise there in industry and technology.

Several amendments to the U.S. Constitution were the direct result of the Civil War. The Thirteenth Amendment, which was ratified, or approved, in 1865, formally ended slavery. The Fourteenth Amendment, ratified in 1868, guaranteed citizenship and related rights to all persons born or naturalized in the United States. And the Fifteenth Amendment, ratified in 1870, declared that a person's right to vote could not be denied based on race, color, or previous condition as a slave.

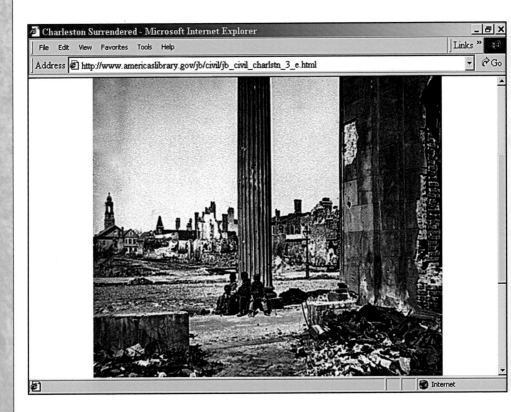

Charleston Surrendered - Microsoft Internet Explorer

File   Edit   View   Favorites   Tools   Help

Links »

Address   http://www.americaslibrary.gov/jb/civil/jb_civil_charlstn_3_e.html   Go

Internet

▲ The city of Charleston, South Carolina, in ruins following the war. It would take years for the South to recover from the war's destruction.

Not all of the differences between North and South that led to the Civil War have truly ended, however. A hundred years after the war, the civil rights movement of the 1960s saw battles of a different kind, as African Americans fought for equal rights in voting and education. The struggle for racial equality that began before the Civil War continues into the twenty-first century. And the question of how much power states should have compared to the power of the federal government continues to be argued.

▶ From War to Remembrance

In 1913, on the fiftieth anniversary of the Battle of Gettysburg, Civil War veterans held a reunion on the famous battlefield. There, white-haired men from both sides met at the stone wall that had once divided them, shaking hands and telling stories like old friends.

The Civil War was an important test of our nation's founding principles of democracy and freedom. Before the war, *United States* was considered a plural term; after the war, *United States* became a singular noun, and the country a single nation. The American Civil War divided the nation as no event has before or since, at a cost in human life that is still difficult to comprehend: Nearly 2 percent of the American population at the time perished. In the end, however, the United States became stronger than it had ever been before.

Chapter Notes

Chapter 1. A Fateful Charge

1. Geoffrey Ward with Ric Burns and Ken Burns, *The Civil War* (New York: Vintage Books, 1994), p. 187.

Chapter 2. The Coming Storm

1. Charles Johnson, Patricia Smith, and the WGBH Series Research Team, *Africans in America: America's Journey through Slavery* (New York: Harcourt Brace & Company, 1998), p. 48.

2. Frederick Douglass and Harriet Jacobs, *Narrative of the Life of Frederick Douglass, A Slave & Incidents in the Life of a Slave Girl* (New York: Modern Library, 2000), p. 17.

3. David Herbert Donald, *Lincoln* (New York: Simon & Schuster, 1995), p. 206.

4. Geoffrey Ward with Ric Burns and Ken Burns, *The Civil War* (New York: Vintage Books, 1994), p. 33.

5. Douglas Southall Freeman, *Lee* (New York: Collier Books, 1993), p. 111.

Chapter 3. War Erupts, 1861–1862

1. Geoffrey Ward with Ric Burns and Ken Burns, *The Civil War* (New York: Vintage Books, 1994), pp. 102–103.

2. Douglas Southall Freeman, *Lee* (New York: Collier Books, 1993), p. 292.

3. David Herbert Donald, *Lincoln* (New York: Simon & Schuster, 1995), p. 407.

Chapter 4. The High-Water Mark, 1863

1. Douglas Southall Freeman, *Lee* (New York: Collier Books, 1993), p. 302.

2. David J. Eicher, *The Longest Night: A Military History of the Civil War* (New York: Simon & Schuster, 2001), p. 529.

3. James M. McPherson, *The Negro's Civil War: How American Blacks Felt and Acted During the War for the Union* (New York: Ballantine Books, 1991), p. 185.

4. Garry Wills, *Lincoln at Gettysburg: The Words that Remade America* (New York: Simon & Schuster, 1992), p. 263.

Chapter 5. The Armies Dig In, 1864–1865

1. Geoffrey Ward with Ric Burns and Ken Burns, *The Civil War* (New York: Vintage Books, 1994), p. 295.

2. Douglas Southall Freeman, *Lee* (New York: Collier Books, 1993), p. 483.

3. James M. McPherson, *Battle Cry of Freedom: The Civil War Era* (New York and Oxford: Oxford University Press, 1988), p. 849.

4. David Herbert Donald, *Lincoln* (New York: Simon & Schuster, 1995), p. 599.

Further Reading

Arnold, James R., and Roberta Wiener. *On to Richmond: The Civil War in the East, 1861–1862.* Minneapolis: Lerner Publishing Group, 2002.

Beller, Susan Provost. *To Hold This Ground: A Desperate Battle of Gettysburg.* New York: Margaret K. McElderry Books, 1995.

Catton, Bruce. *The American Heritage New History of the Civil War.* New York: Penguin Books, 1996.

Diouf, Sylviane A. *Growing Up in Slavery.* Brookfield, Conn.: Millbrook Press, 2001.

Foote, Shelby. *The Civil War: A Narrative* (Three volumes). New York: Vintage Books, 1986.

Gallagher, Gary W. *Lee and His Army in Confederate History.* Chapel Hill: University of North Carolina Press, 2001.

Heinrichs, Ann. *The Emancipation Proclamation.* Minneapolis: Compass Point Books, 2002.

Johnson, Charles, Patricia Smith, and the WGBH Series Research Team. *Africans in America: America's Journey through Slavery.* New York: Harcourt Brace & Company, 1998.

McPherson, James M. *Battle Cry of Freedom: The Civil War Era.* New York and Oxford: Oxford University Press, 1988.

Schraff, Anne E. *Frederick Douglass: Speaking Out Against Slavery.* Berkeley Heights, N.J.: Enslow Publishers, Inc., 2001.